HAPPINISM

HAPPINISM

A Goal for All Humanity

Howard O. Eaton, Ph.D.

Sometime Senior Economic Analyst, Department of Commerce, and at the American Embassy, Ankara

EXPOSITION PRESS   HICKSVILLE, NEW YORK

To Marie

CONTENTS

HAPPINISM

A NEW DECLARATION

For two hundred years we in the United States have enjoyed the "inalienable" right to the pursuit of happiness—but for most of us this has remained an empty phrase and a frustrated pursuit, with more misery than happiness. Why? What went wrong?

All the nostalgia of a Bicentennial will not give us the answer. 1776 solved one great problem—it put an end to the rapacity of kings on this continent. But it left many other problems untouched and unsolved. A few score gentlemen did what they could; they won political independence with the help of Washington and his Continentals and an alliance with the King of France.

Some of those who sat in the Continental Congress were slave owners who prated about liberty and equality, but kept their slaves. They founded a government that had no room for Indians not taxed and for the "three fourths of other persons."

Since then the two hundred years of American history have been written for the most part in blood, much of it spilled in senseless and selfish quarrels. The Civil War not only killed several hundred thousand brave men on both sides of the conflict, but its monetary cost was greater than it would have cost to have bought every slave at the going auction price of 1860 and to have freed them all by a stroke of the pen. And the money paid for them would have provided an ample capital for industrializing the South, equipping it with new railroads, harbors, highways, and factories, and for providing a decent education for the freedmen.

America's shameless treatment of the Indians bordered on genocide. The buffalo were slaughtered on the great plains in order to starve the Indians into submission. All through American history from Lexington and Bunker Hill to Vietnam blood has flowed. Let us have done with such butchery. And the history of Europe has been equally bloody, or more so.

Senseless and wasteful war is not our only problem. The industrial nations have had their history pockmarked with depressions, famines, lynching and violence. Even today the whole industrial world is beset with inflation, unemployment, exorbitant interest rates, widespread misery. And the non-industrial nations are only now slowly emerging from the ruthless exploitation of colonialism.

A few score men signed the Declaration of 1776. We today, men and women, must now look to the future more than to the past. A new Declaration is in order, that we all take a high resolve that collectively we will put an end to these ancient miseries and futilities. We must dismiss the pessimism which sneers at any such effort. We must face the future with confidence that all our goals can be achieved if enough of us agree on what our major goals are and on the manner in which we will work together to achieve them.

A NEW MAYFLOWER COMPACT

American history did not begin in 1776. Over a hundred and fifty years before that date, heroic men and women faced a bleak and forbidding wilderness in which they hoped to build their new homes. While the *Mayflower* rode at anchor in Plymouth Bay, in 1620, her crew and passengers (the "Saints and Strangers") looked out at the wintry landscape of a new land. They realized that they had left once and for all the security of organized society back in England and Holland. If they were to have again this same security and comfort in this new land they must establish it themselves, by their own deed and act. And so, before they set foot on this new land they drew up and signed a Compact, known in history as the Mayflower Compact.

Like those tough-minded Pilgrims of long ago we today must make the same effort. We must draw up and sign a new compact as our guide and security while we set foot on this new land of our own future, a future bright with the promise of peace and prosperity for all, but menaced by greed, the fear of atomic war, plagued with overpopulation, ignorance, disease, pollution and plutocracy.

It is important that this new compact be carefully worded, subject to amendment according to its own provisions, and complete in all essentials. We cannot expect large numbers of people to agree to a vague, incomplete or misleading compact. This adequacy and precision of our compact cannot be reached at a single bound. All we can hope to achieve here is to suggest the main lines along which those of us who are in substantial agreement with the present book can work together in drafting and publishing a compact which will serve our purpose.

The problems we face are enormous and complex. They cannot be solved by doctrinaires, by dictators, by rigid ideologies, or by turning everything over to an all-powerful government. What we here propose is a many-sided organization that can deal with these problems effectively one by one in a democratic manner, an organization in which we all can take a part each after his or her interests and abilities, each of us offering his or her best ideas for the consideration of all of us.

It is not the purpose of the present book to offer anything more than very general suggestions as to the detailed solution of these many problems. We leave this to a subsequent book or sequel to be discussed later on. Our problem here is to outline ways in which all citizens who are concerned about these problems or any of them can work together in a democratic manner to arrive at acceptable and effective solutions.

Let us think of the present book as a vessel specially built for our collective voyage into the future, fitted for our joint search for the safe haven where mankind will be assured of worldwide peace and an economy of abundance for all people everywhere. The vessel alone cannot be the safe haven we seek. But without it we cannot even embark on such a voyage.

Our present task is to inspire the toiling masses of mankind with the hope that we offer here a vessel sturdy and well keeled for this voyage, strong enough to withstand the buffetings of violent storms of passion and greed, piloted by well-trained seamen, and guided in all the cross-currents of opinion by the democratic process. All disputed matters must be submitted to a referendum in which all who are in agreement with our common purpose and have signed our compact will have a vote.

Those who embark on this new *Mayflower* must have the assurance that they will have priority in the enjoyment of the economy of abundance under the banner of world peace and security, which are the goals we seek. These motives will furnish the fuel for propelling our new *Mayflower* on this long voyage. All who would seek to be passengers on this voyage must be willing to sign our new compact when it has been prepared.

Our new compact must fully protect the human dignity of all signers regardless of their race, sex, religion or nationality. The problems which confront us are worldwide in scope, and therefore we must seek the support of all persons everywhere. We call our joint effort "Happinism" and all who subscribe to our goals and methods of reaching them will be known as "Happinists." Happinism will be able to reach and convince people of every class and walk of life through the efforts of trained agents, who will be able to make it clear to all that happinism answers our most urgent questions with carefully reasoned answers.

We can summarize briefly our happinist purpose by saying that it is an attempt to find a viable compromise between (a) efficient planning and direction of our joint economic, social and political life and (b) the protection of personal freedom.

Dictatorships and totalitarian systems of the right or left claim to achieve efficiency (and "make the trains run on time") —but they sneer at personal liberty and freedom of the individual. By contrast, laissez-faire free enterprise is theoretically built on freedom of the individual, but is limited in fact to an unrestricted freedom of the winners in the competitive struggle and their enjoyment of such profits as they can command, with scant regard for the freedom and welfare of the rest of us.

Happinism frankly admits that these problems are enormous—but happinism is built on a method to seek the solution of these problems in a democratic manner such that the ultimate solution of these problems will never jeopardize the freedom of each and all of us. At this early stage we do not pretend to be able to say what these solutions will be. We are concerned here with the method of reaching concensus as to the solutions of these problems. We leave it to this method to reach these solutions by a democratic process. And no critic has the right to say that he knows what we "are aiming at." All we ask is that critics confine their attack to this method we here propose.

3

THE ORGANIZATION
OF HAPPINISM

Happinism is the organized effort of all happinists everywhere to achieve the happiness of each happinist wherever he or she may be. The chief problems of our times are world problems. We emphasize the word *achieve*; it is not enough to say we have the right to pursue happiness. We will be satisfied only with achievement.

Furthermore we insist on a specific numerical criterion: any happinist compact will be fully valid and binding on its signers only if at least three-fourths of the adult citizens in at least five nations having each a population of 30,000,000 persons (or more) agree to it. We set this as a minimum goal. That the happinist effort will be sterile and futile if supported by a smaller number is a simple statement of fact. There have been too many idealistic movements that started with only a small fraction of the population in agreement—and remained essentially futile. Only if we have the committed support of three-fourths of the adult population in the principal nations will we be able to achieve the major portion of our program.

Furthermore happinism must have adequate financial support. It must not be reduced to holding a tin cup or passing the hat. Any individual who is unwilling to make every year an annual contribution based on the character and size of his or her income is not eligible to be a happinist. Happinism makes a distinction between earned income and investment income. The rate of contribution from earned income begins at a very low figure, namely,

1/10 of 1 percent of after-tax income up to $10,000 (or the equivalent in other currencies), and 1 percent of after-tax income up to $50,000. (Any income over $50,000 will be considered to be investment income.) The rate of expected contribution from investment income will begin at 5% of the first $10,000 of after-tax income, 10% of the next $10,000, 15% of the next increment of $10,000 and so on. The investment income of senior citizens (up to $50,000) will be considered to be earned income.

Happinism cannot accept any gift, donation, or subsidy from any person who is not a happinist, or from any corporation or group not under happinist control. Will there be any "cheating" or "underestimating" of one's income for purposes of calculating one's expected contribution? There is this risk, of course, but if circumstances warrant, the given individual may re requested to discuss the matter with a happinist agent. If this offends the person involved we would be better off without his contribution.

As soon as possible an organizing committee will be formed and will be able to: (1) Provide for the incorporation of Happinism as Happinism, Inc. The papers of incorporation will specify that the actions of the corporation must be in accordance with the provisions of the present book, and that these provisions may be modified or amended only by majority approval of all happinists voting in a referendum arranged for the purpose of approving or disapproving any proposed amendment.

(2) The organizing committee will also make arrangements for a national headquarters, for employing a staff, and for opening and maintaining one or more bank accounts to receive the contributions of individual happinists. All financial records of Happinism, Inc., will be audited and verified by an independent firm of public accountants and will be published annually.

(3) One of the duties of the staff will be to provide each happinist with an appropriate certificate (e.g., a wallet card) certifying his or her agreement to the principles of happinism expressed in this book together with the date of such agreement as fixed by a signature. The staff will also keep a record of names and addresses of happinists together with relevant information.

The first ten happinists living in any one city or county are expected to form a local happinist committee. Each local committee will elect one of its members to serve on the state or provincial committee, and as soon as there are ten or more members of this committee, a delegate to the national committee will be chosen. Likewise when there are ten or more members of the national committee they will choose a delegate to the World Happinist Council, which will be formally organized for business when there are at least ten delegates sitting in it.

This pyramidal structure is not intended to serve for more than a year or so. The democratic principle requires that all of the seats on these various committees, after a full year of operation, shall be filled by elections by secret ballot and that all happinists resident in any such locality or nation shall each have a vote. The Council may provide more definite rules and regulations for all such elections.

After payment of the expenses of organizing and operating the various committees mentioned above, the available funds in the happinist treasury shall be distributed as follows: 30% to the local committees, 30% to the state or provincial committees, 20% to the several national committees, and the remaining 20% to the World Council. Actual amounts to be distributed in accordance with this schedule shall be determined by the Executive Committee specified in the charter of Happinism, Inc., until the Council is formally organized; thereafter all such matters will be decided by the

Council. So far as may be the amounts distributed to each particular committee will be proportional to the population of the locality, district or nation concerned. The primary purpose to be served by these funds shall be to inform the public as to the goals and programs of Happinism and to persuade as many persons as possible to become happinists.

Each committee shall inform its constituents of proposed actions and if a referendum is demanded by one-fourth of the committee or 5% of its constituents then the referendum shall be promptly held as a guide to the committee. Not every happinist will wish to be consulted on the details of happinist action. Those happinists who do wish to be consulted will be urged to join one of the following panels:

Panel A—concerned with the extractive industries such as agriculture, fishing, hunting, mining, and the oil and gas industry and with the ethical management of each such industry and the impact of such an industry on the ecology of the total human environment and the problems of conservation of natural resources, and related questions.

Panel B—concerned with manufacturing and processing industries and the ethical problems involved, including problems of quality control.

Panel C—concerned with finance and commerce, banking and credit, and the distribution of products and services in an ethical manner with a view to maintaining stability and the lessening of the impact of inflation and speculation.

Panel D—concerned with human welfare, including medical care and public health, education, unemployment, alcoholism and drug addiction, and the long range problems of overpopulation and family planning; together with the alleviation of human misery wherever possible, all in the light of ethics.

Panel E—concerned with government and politics and

happinist participation in political action on an ethical basis, as described below.

Panel F—concerned with the problems of ethics, morality, and related matters, and the human right of every person to life, liberty, personal dignity, the ownership of personal property, and the achievement of individual happiness of all in a peaceful and prosperous world.

Any happinist who joins one of these six panels will be known as a participant. Each panel will elect a chairman and an editorial committee of not more than, say, ten panelists.

4

THE HAPPINIST PROGRAM

The primary function of the six panels is to prepare the text of the sequel of this book, to be called *The Happinist Program*. The preparation of this text will require extensive research, careful formulation, debate between panelists who have differing views on any question, culminating in editorial decisions by the elected editorial committee. The Council may designate an editor-in-chief to coordinate the work of the several panel committees; if necessary the editor-in-chief may appoint a general editorial committee consisting of representatives from each of the panels. Whenever practicable any controversial matters shall be resolved by questionnaires circulated to the panel or panels involved. Every participant will be expected to respond to any questionnaires from the panel chairman. Final preparation of the text of *The Happinist Program* must be guided by the results of these questionnaires.

There is no shortage of good ideas and viable plans for *The Happinist Program*. What is needed is to find a democratic and efficient method for integrating many such ideas into a single, unified and widely acceptable whole, so that everyone will know that this is the definitive program. If there is serious disagreement within the Council concerning any controversial matter, the Council may call for a general referendum and all happinists (not merely the panelists or participants chiefly concerned) will have a vote. Only if the referendum approves the proposed text will final authorization be granted by the Council to proceed with publication.

All happinists will be expected to guide their actions by *The Happinist Program*, although no happinist renounces his or her right to propose amendments either to the present book or to its sequel. Proposed amendments will be submitted to a panel for study and eventual action, and if there be serious controversy on it in the Council it may be submitted for a referendum.

To begin with there will be one delegate in the Council elected by each national committee. We must, however, provide adequate representation for active participants in the Council, the people who are actively engaged in the development of the happinist program. To meet this need each participant may select another participant to hold his or her proxy for the ensuing year, and any such designated participant who holds at least 1,000 proxies will have a seat in the Council for the following year.

We must take care that the Council shall not become so large as to be ineffective. The ideal maximum size for such a deliberative body is in the neighborhood of 300 members. Therefore if it appears likely that the Council might exceed 300 members for any subsequent year, the qualifying number of proxies necessary for Council membership will be appropriately increased. The Council will make this decision and will provide proxy forms for the selection of proxy-members so as to protect the confidential character of this selection.

To prevent the domination of the Council by members from one or two of the larger nations, not more than 4 percent of the total membership of the Council should be citizens of any one nation having a population in excess of 200 million people; not more than 2 percent of the Council membership should be citizens of any nation having a population of more than 25 million people but less than

200 million people; and not more than 1 percent of the Council membership should be citizens of any nation having a population of less than 25 million people. This will provide a good balance all around.

We may assume that a fairly large fraction of the total population would find it difficult to study and understand all aspects of happinism. The Council may therefore authorize local committees to employ persons skilled in explaining such matters; they will be able to make happinism understandable and acceptable to most of the persons they are able to reach. These persons will be known as "advocates" of happinism and will receive appropriate remuneration.

The various panels mentioned above will assist these agents and others interested in suggesting how an economy of abundance can be obtained. Such explanations will necessarily be offered only in general terms without specific predictions as to the detailed method by which happinism will actually achieve its goals. Emphasis will always be placed on the condition that happinism can assuredly achieve its goals *only* if the total number of happinists is greater than three-fourths of the adult population. This may appear to some to be a large order, but any attempt to achieve the large goals of happinism (world peace, national security, and an economy of abundance for all everywhere) if the number of happinists is less than we here demand would inevitably lead to futility, total loss of credibility, widespread disappointment.

5

HAPPINIST ECONOMICS

Modern economics is very complex. By analogy we might compare the operation of a free enterprise economy to steering a "Blackhound" bus. A blackhound bus differs from a Greyhound bus in that every passenger's seat is equipped with a steering wheel. Those passengers who want the bus to turn to the right turn their wheel accordingly, and the other passengers who want the bus to go to the left turn their wheels in that direction. At the front of the bus there is an analog computer which receives the impulses from all the steering wheels and averages them out to determine the direction the bus is to move. Those who turned their wheels too far in the wrong direction are thrown off the bus—and sometimes the bus itself runs into difficulties.

Our free enterprise economy operates in much the same manner; our analog computer is the price system, which determines the market price as the result of the "dollar votes" of all producers and consumers. It is a good system for those who don't get thrown off the bus because they made bad choices. But far too many people get thrown off the bus, with much needless misery. Happinism offers the hope that this system can be improved so that there will be less misery and more prosperity for all. Certain changes will have to be made. The trouble is that there are powerful and wealthy minorities who benefit enormously from the lurching and erratic twisting of the bus. It is impossible, therefore, for happinism to specify how the present system is to be corrected as long as happinism has enrolled only a minority of the population.

There are a great many businesses in the free enterprise system that suffer very much because of the fluctuations and ups and downs of the economy. It is difficult if not impossible to make sound plans or long-range decisions in such a roller-coaster type of economy. Happinism will find very vigorous support for its efforts to stabilize the economy, to minimize and in the end to put an end to inflation— or its equally devastating sequel, deflation and "price collapse."

As the number of happinists grows the power of happinism's appeal to sanity in the conduct of free enterprise business will greatly increase. Business firms that realize the benefits they will obtain from a more stabilized economy will be eager to be known as "happinist enterprises." Such an enterprise must be free from the taint of monopoly or oligopoly, it must be operated in accordance with ethical principles, and with the aim of assisting in the achievement of the goals of happinism (peace, prosperity, stability); it should be able to offer a good return for its owners, while guaranteeing a satisfactory income for its employees and a fair price for its products and services. Every happinist enterprise will have the right to employ the trade-marked symbols of happinism in displaying, packaging, and distributing its products and services. This may constitute a marketing aid of enormous value as the total number of happinists increases.

The several panels mentioned above, particularly Panels B, C and F, will provide the necessary guidance in granting to any private enterprise the right to the title "happinist enterprise." There will be urgent need to formulate an ethical code valid for all happinists and happinist enterprises. In the employment and personnel policies of any happinist enterprise it should be clear that preference will be given to the employment and promotion of happinists who have subscribed to the ethical code with due regard to the date on which the code was accepted. This means that Johnny-Come-Lately may find that some of the more desirable employment opportunities will go to others with a higher priority. Most people will readily understand the equity of such a provision and also the desirability of being an early-bird rather than waiting.

One essential duty of every happinist is to provide the local committee or agent with the names and addresses of his relatives and friends and the promise that he will assist in the task of explaining happinism to them. The local committee and agent will then provide these persons with further materials and an urgent invitation to become happinists also.

6

HAPPINIST POLITICS

Happinism must necessarily concern itself with the political life of the locality, the state or province, and the nation—and ultimately the world. It will be the duty of Panel E to study this matter, and to suggest detailed plans by which happinists can work together in this field. The main point to keep in mind is that happinism must not be partisan, that neither the Republican Party nor the Democratic Party (or any other party) should be able to take exclusive possession of happinism and turn it into a football of politics.

Every happinist will be expected to register his political affiliation or preference with the local committee or agent. Well in advance of an election, the state, provincial or national committee will determine (by questionnaire or polling) who is the candidate among the Republican candidates who is preferred by most Republican happinists and likewise who is the preferred Democratic happinist candidate. At the primary election all Republican happinists will be expected to support the Republican happinist candidate and similarly on the Democratic side. If the two preferred happinist candidates (a Republican and a Democrat) have won their respective primaries, then we can feel reasonably sure that it will be a happinist who wins the general election. If, however, only one of the happinist candidates won in the primaries (either the Republican or the Democrat), then all happinists voters would be expected to support this happinist candidate even if it means crossing party lines.

Panel F (in cooperation with Panel E) will be expected to prepare an ethical code for public officers which all happinists desiring to be candidates for public office (either elected or appointed) will be expected to sign and adhere to. This code will specifically prohibit any unethical practices now altogether too common in politics and public life, such as nepotism, corruption, "graft," influence peddling, conflict of interest, and so forth. Panel F will also be responsible for providing fair and equitable methods for promptly ascertaining if any signatory of this code is guilty of violation of it, or even open to a reasonable doubt on the matter. It will be much easier to enforce an ethical code of this character which has been voluntarily signed by all candidates than to enforce any statutory provisions entailing complex and lengthy legal procedures. The burden of proof will be on any person who has signed the code to demonstrate that any specific action complained of is clearly not of an unethical character. Any public figure who is unwilling to maintain a record and a reputation as spotless as Caesar's wife should not sign this code. This principle will serve to rebuild the credibility of politicians and politics.

One very firm provision of the code must prohibit any effort to "split the happinist vote" in favor of an overly ambitious politician unwilling to accept the designation of a rival as the "preferred happinist candidate." There will be only one "preferred happinist candidate" in the primary election of any party, and only one happinist candidate on the ticket of either party in a general election. Panel F will have ample authority to look into any such situation and to prevent the use of the happinist insignia by any rival of the preferred happinist candidate. Panel F may even go so far, if need be, as to declare that such a maverick candidate is no longer a happinist.

All happinists will be expected to do whatever party work is necessary for the benefit of happinist candidates of their party. If happinism has succeeded in enlisting a large percentage of the adult population, then there should be little difficulty for happinist candidates to win in the election.

7

SOLUTIONS TO
WORLD PROBLEMS

After happinists have been elected or appointed to office we have the right to expect that they will be loyal to the goals and principles of happinism, as expressed either in *The Happinist Program,* in the work of Panel F, Panel E, or elsewhere. This does not mean that an elected legislator or executive or an appointed official who is a happinist is bound in every respect. It is specifically understood and agreed that every such happinist shall retain complete freedom of speech, action and voting concerning other matters not clearly contained in the happinist literature. There are many questions of public life which will not be clearly decided by the happinist literature or procedure. Such questions will remain the normal subject of political action and partisan debate. Happinism is not to be a blanket covering everything. We must still retain the benefits of the two-party system. There can still be normal political rivalry and debate within the happinist structure between happinist Republicans and happinist Democrats. Only when a particular issue has been resolved by discussion and questionnaires within the six panels and if need be by referendum in which all happinists will have a vote will such an issue become a clearly stated happinist principle to which all happinists must accede.

In other words happinism is not concerned with a great many of the questions and problems of local affairs, social questions, city or county government, state or provincial politics, or national issues which are the particular problem of a particular nation. Happinism is primarily devoted to the search for solutions of worldwide problems that transcend national boundaries and for the solution of which there does not now exist any adequate means for dealing with them. And it is these great problems which sweep across all local and national boundaries and render any attempt to deal with their local or national aspects futile. In very many cases the efforts of national governments to deal with the purely national aspects of such problems only result in tariff wars, currency devaluations, and other forms of national rivalry and chauvinistic braggadocio. All too frequently this has been the seedbed of military bluster, saber rattling and eventually war.

These problems are not simple, and their solution is not to be found in political slogans or personal ambition. Any one who mounts a stump or a horse, waves his hat and shouts "Follow ME" is a childish and dangerous demagogue. We cannot leave the answer to these questions to some plutocratic multinational corporation seeking only its own profit in the troubled waters, and even willing to trouble the waters for its own advantage. These are world problems and the peoples of all the nations of the world have a right to a voice in their solution.

It will be the duty of the participants working together within the framework of the six panels mentioned above to seek the solution of these problems. The solution of these problems on a world level will generally involve the concomitant solution of the local aspects of these same problems within the economies of the participating nations. Only those nations can be considered participating nations capable of benefiting from these worldwide solutions that are nations in which three-fourths of the adult population have become happinists. Not all happinists will be participants actively engaged in the work of seeking the solution of these problems. Any happinist who wants to be a participant can choose the panel with which he or she wishes to cooperate. A person who is not a happinist will not be eligible to be a participant. Participants will not be expected or obligated to make any financial or other contribution to happinism except what they give as happinists. In many cases participants who have contributed research or materials to the solution of one or another of these problems will be appropriately remunerated.

It will be only when the work of the six panels converges into the formulation and editing of a single unified book, *The Happinist Program,* that the nature of the happinist solutions to these problems will emerge. As we have said before, this book will be the product of a strictly democratic process in which all personal opinions and collective thinking will have had a fair opportunity to be heard and compared with other opinions. And one of the chief features of this procedure is that all the participants engaged in it will have voluntarily accepted a common code of ethics. Some of these participants will be active politicians and elected legislators or officials; some of them will be academic and technical experts in a given field; some of them will be active and successful businessmen and women. All of the ideas and plans which they offer to one of the panels will be treated alike; the editorial staff of the panel will prepare these ideas and plans in the form of brief and succinct memoranda for distribution to the specialists in the panel who will evaluate them and if need be circulate questionnaires to determine the acceptability of the idea.

This procedure is fundamentally different from the process today by which rival politicians sketch very briefly their individual ideas and plans for solving many different problems, and then beg for votes which will put them in office with the mandate to do what they can along the lines they suggest. These rival plans clash on the floor of the legislative body, and what results is generally an unsatisfactory watered-down compromise. A legislative body is simply not a good place to work out a complicated solution to a difficult problem. The happinist method has the distinct advantage that all its ideas and plans have been submitted to objective and impartial scrutiny by disinterested experts, combed over by penetrating questionnaires to which many participants will give answers, and ultimately voted on by all happinists in a referendum. When such a happinist proposal is presented to a legislative body for final approval it will not be a political football of rival factions. The legislative body may reject it and send it back for further study and revision, and this might result in a definite improvement. When it comes back for reconsideration in its revised form it may very well be still better.

8

A UNIVERSAL CODE
OF ETHICS

The fact that all participants will have accepted and signed a common code of ethics may raise questions in some minds. What is the coercive force which will compel individual participants to obey this code? To ask this question is to reveal a misunderstanding of the nature of ethics. There is nothing coercive about ethics. Persons who desire to be ethical will subscribe willingly to the code. Failure to "obey" the code will not be punished coercively. Such a failure, if verified by appropriate investigation, will simply be followed by having one's signature expunged from the record. That is all. It is the way to make sure that no known violator of the code can continue to be, or pretend to be, a participant.

For instance, one of the necessary and fundamental requirements of the code for participants must be that all of them agree not to publish or make public in any way any part or aspect of the work of the panel prior to its final publication after full approval of all concerned. Violation of this obligation could spell disaster to the work of the panel. Premature publication of the work of the panel might serve the personal ambition of one of the participants, eager to win public approbation and possibly win an election. Obviously such a premature publication would be unethical and would damage or violate the rights of the many other participants who had worked on the problem.

Therefore any participant who violates this stricture of the code would be promptly denied the right to call himself or herself a participant.

Whether a person who has been ejected from the ranks of participants should be allowed to seek reinstatement as a participant is a question which would have to be referred to the Council with a full statement of all the relevant facts. Of course a person who finds the work of being a participant too onerous or unsatisfactory would be allowed to withdraw from participation at any time, with full right to reenter the ranks of participants later on.

It may be helpful if we indicate briefly some of the other obligations of an ethical character which will presumably be required of all participants, and even of all happinists. These suggested obligations are sketched here to furnish a basis for discussion.

No participant or happinist should ever use force in any form, or even recommend the use of force, violence, or coercion against any other person for any purpose whatever (other than in self-defense against an overt aggression threatening life or serious physical injury, but not loss of property).

This fundamental rule of non-violence must be thought of as extending to nations in the field of international relations. No happinist shall ever recommend or support the employment of force or violence by one's own nation against any other nation or the citizens thereof (except, of course, in resistance to invasion or aggression by any other nation or its citizens). The rule for the outlawing of force and violence between nations will have to be embodied in a multilateral treaty between participating nations which will make even the advocacy of the use of violence against another participating nation a statutory felony punishable by imprisonment. It must be clearly stated, however, that the use of force against a non-participating nation which is guilty of threatening to use force or violence is permitted. As long as there are non-participating nations heavily armed and prone to threats of violence, the happinists living in participating nations must be willing to spend tax money for maintaining a powerful defense establishment fully able to protect against any such violence.

No happinist should support, propose, urge, recommend, or vote for the use of the power and police force of his own nation to obtain economic or similar benefits and advantages for the citizens and businesses of his own nation to the detriment and economic disadvantage of the citizens of another participating nation. Existing tariffs and other trade barriers may be permitted to remain until it is possible to diminish or remove them by reciprocal agreements with other nations. But they must not be increased.

No happinist shall fail in any wise to respect fully the dignity or the personal or civil rights of any other person (whether happinist or not), particularly if such other person be a member of a racial or cultural minority or a believer in a religious creed different from the religious creed of the said happinist. No happinist shall urge, support, or consent to any discrimination against any person (s) on the basis of sex, heredity, national or cultural origin or antecedents, racial characteristics, age or religious belief. It is very important to state these requirements very fully; any happinist who commits any act contrary to what is here clearly stated to be the obligations of a happinist or who in any circumstance uses language to encourage or justify any such violation of the code of ethics of happinism should be summarily brought to the attention of the proper committee of Panel F—and if Panel F finds that there has been a violation of the code then the person in question should be deprived of the right to claim to be a happinist.

It is also quite obvious that no happinist should be guilty of perjury, mendacity, prevarication, untruth, or any falsehood or misrepresentation, or any form of pornography, drug abuse, excessive use of alcoholic beverages, or refusal of treatment or assistance to remedy any such addiction. Happinists should certainly avoid any form of unsocial or antisocial activity or exploitation of human weakness for personal gain; this would include, among other and related or similar rackets, prostitution, procurement, gambling, "the numbers," loan sharking, kidnapping, and corruption of the police and judiciary.

Happinists are under obligation to assist law enforcement officials in the arrest, prosecution and conviction of criminals who are guilty of the antisocial behavior here mentioned.

9

SUMMARY

In summary, the principal purpose of this book is to offer a method by which the large majority of the citizens of the free world can work together harmoniously and effectively in achieving (not merely pursuing) the happiness of each by achieving the happiness of all. We do not offer a panacea or an ideology. We do not believe that the achievement of universal happiness can be delegated to a few dictators or leaders, or to a man on horseback. If the vast majority of the citizens who would be the beneficiaries of this program are unwilling to make the relatively small effort required of each of them as individuals then this plan must fail.

We are not so pessimistic; if each one helps one the plan will succeed.

The first step to take by any person willing to become a happinist is for him or her to sign a statement in his or her own words in agreement with the provisions of this book. This would imply willingness to be governed by these provisions. Such a signed statement should then be sent to the author or to the publisher. It is this act of signing which is crucial.

During the First World War Georges Clemenceau growled, "A drop of oil is worth a drop of blood." Has oil gone up in price? Is blood cheaper? Let us change the bargain to read: A drop of ink is worth a drop of blood. Let us put the ink at the tip of our pens to sign this agreement and stop the flow of blood.

*　　*　　*

In the confidence that happinism will be a benefit to all mankind I subscribe to the ethical code contained herein and pledge that I will, to the best of my ability, be faithful to its provisions.

HOWARD O. EATON